What Is the Story of Frankenstein?

What Is the Story of Frankenstein?

by Sheila Keenan

illustrated by David Malan

Penguin Workshop

For Paula and Iggy—SK

To my monsters, Emmett and Calvin—DM

PENGUIN WORKSHOP
An Imprint of Penguin Random House LLC, New York

©2019 Universal Studios. Frankenstein is a trademark and copyright of Universal Studios. Licensed by Universal Studios Licensing LLLP. All Rights Reserved. Published by Penguin Workshop, an imprint of Penguin Random House LLC, New York. PENGUIN and PENGUIN WORKSHOP are trademarks of Penguin Books Ltd. WHO HQ & Design is a registered trademark of Penguin Random House LLC. Printed in the USA.

Visit us online at www. penguinrandomhouse.com.

Library of Congress Cataloging-in-Publication Data is available upon request.

ISBN 9781524788421 (paperback)   10 9 8 7 6 5 4 3 2
ISBN 9781524788438 (library binding)   10 9 8 7 6 5 4 3 2 1

Contents

What Is the Story of Frankenstein?

On May 17, 2014, a curious crowd streamed into a big, open plaza in Geneva, Switzerland. They circled a mysterious figure that was nearly eight feet tall. It was completely covered in white, bandage-like cloths. Pillars topped with metal coils stood on either side of the figure.

Silently, three men removed the draped cloths.

Suddenly, bolts of electricity shot out from the tops of the pillars, zapping the figure in between them. A spotlight lit up the statue.

The crowd gasped. They were face-to-face with a horrifying bronze giant. The head of the statue was gnarled and twisted. Long, jagged scars crisscrossed its chest. Its large hands dangled from wrists that were covered in bracelets of stitches. One hand was curled. It looked like it could reach out and grab you. Even scarier: Its eyes stared straight into yours—and the monster appeared to be walking forward!

Behold! *Frankie, a.k.a. The Creature of Doctor Frankenstein.*

This modern sculpture celebrates Frankenstein, one of the most famous monsters of all time. Most people have heard about this dangerous creature that was brought to life by a mad scientist. Many of them have seen the monster in movies or worn a Frankenstein costume for Halloween.

The members of KLAT, the Swiss artist group that created the sculpture, were being playful when they called their work "Frankie." The rest of the statue's name, "The Creature of Doctor Frankenstein," is more accurate.

The creature is a fictional character in a book that is more than two hundred years old. It does not have a name in that story. Then who is Frankenstein? He is the young science student in the story whose experiments created the monster.

Today, more people know about the monster than the book. What may really surprise them is that the Frankenstein story was the idea of a teenage girl. She wrote it on a dare! And it really *was* a dark and stormy night when young Mary Shelley started writing . . .

CHAPTER 1
A Spooky Contest

The summer of 1816 was a rainy one at Lake Geneva in Switzerland. Day after day, the guests at a beautiful lakeside house called Villa Diodati were stuck inside. (*Villa* is the Italian word for a large country house.) They read books and wrote poetry. They discussed science, literature, and philosophy. One stormy evening, they read spooky stories aloud. Their host suggested a contest for his guests: Everyone should write a ghost story.

Mary Wollstonecraft Godwin started thinking.

She was a guest at one of the most famous house parties in literary history. The host at the villa was the English poet and nobleman George Gordon Byron. (He was known as Lord Byron.) Mary had eloped with another British poet, Percy Bysshe Shelley. Her stepsister was with them. So was Byron's personal doctor. They were all young and passionate about the arts, science, and nature. They lived in a world of ideas and not necessarily rules.

The Year Without a Summer

How does an Indonesian volcano bring rain to a Swiss villa?

By erupting.

Villa Diodati near Lake Geneva is almost ten thousand miles away from Mount Tambora in what is now Indonesia. On April 10, 1815, the Mount Tambora volcano blew. It is the largest volcanic eruption in recorded history. Thousands and thousands of people died. Volcanic ash, dust, and gases spread throughout the atmosphere. By 1816, the weather in Europe and North America had been affected. There were terrific rainstorms with thunder and lightning. There was snow, frost, and freezing temperatures . . . in the summer! Crops failed. People and animals sickened and starved. For many, it was a year without a summer.

Mary Godwin was the daughter of two radical thinkers. Her mother, Mary Wollstonecraft, had written a book about the recent French Revolution. She also wrote one of the first important books to argue for women's rights and equality. Mary's father, William Godwin, was a

philosopher, author, and publisher. He often wrote about political justice and government reform. Both her parents were well known in Europe.

Mary Wollstonecraft died ten days after her daughter was born on August 30, 1797. Young Mary was mostly raised by her father. He believed she should be well educated. Mary read history, Romantic poetry, gothic novels, the classics, and many books in her father's library. She spent hours writing her own stories. She listened in when scientists, writers, politicians, and intellectuals came to visit her father. And she fell in love with one of those visitors, Percy Bysshe Shelley. They met secretly at her mother's grave.

Percy Bysshe Shelley and Mary Wollstonecraft Godwin became a couple even though he was already married. Percy and Mary led a complicated, but creative life together. They

encouraged each other as writers. They read and
edited each other's work. They traveled, shared
books and new ideas, and wrote a journal together.

Mary in her father's library

But they often didn't have enough money. Mary became pregnant. And their families disapproved of their relationship.

By the time Percy, Mary, and their young son arrived at Lake Geneva, Mary was calling herself Mrs. Shelley. They were delighted to spend time in such a beautiful place with a famous poet such as Lord Byron. The villa was filled with lively conversations, and the ghost-story challenge was thrilling.

Mary Shelley   Percy Bysshe Shelley

But Mary had a hard time thinking of a
story idea for the contest. Days passed: nothing.
Then one night she had a terrifying dream. She
pictured a young man kneeling by "the thing he
had put together." She saw this "hideous corpse"
which the man had "awakened" stir and open its
"yellow, watery" eyes.

She had her story.

The Guest List, Villa Diodati, 1816

George Gordon Byron, Lord Byron (1788–1824) is one of England's greatest poets. He is famous for long Romantic works like *Don Juan*. Because of scandals about his many affairs, he was also famous for being "mad, bad, and dangerous to know." He died of fever during the Greek war for independence, which he supported. The word *Byronic* is used to describe someone moody, passionate, and heroic.

Percy Bysshe Shelley (1792–1822) is also a very famous British poet and writer. His influential poems, like *Adonais*, are deeply spiritual and emotional. Shelley married Mary Wollstonecraft Godwin on December 30, 1816, after his first wife died. They had several children together, but only one son survived. Shelley drowned when a sudden storm sank the boat he was sailing.

Dr. John Polidori (1795–1821) traveled through Europe as Lord Byron's doctor. For the contest, he came up with a story called "The Vampyre." It is sometimes referred to as the first vampire story in English.

Claire (also Clara or Mary Jane) Clairmont (1798–1879) often traveled with the Shelleys. Her mother married William Godwin. She and Mary were stepsisters. She had a daughter with Lord Byron, named Allegra. Claire did not write a ghost story that summer.

CHAPTER 2
Mary Shelley Writes a Book

The story Mary Shelley dreamed up that rainy summer became her famous novel, *Frankenstein; or, The Modern Prometheus*. At the center of her story is Victor Frankenstein, a student of both medieval and modern science. Victor becomes obsessed with "the change from life to death, and death to life." He locks himself away in a laboratory and begins secret experiments. He builds an eight-foot creature from dead human and animal parts. When he manages to bring it to life, Victor is horrified by what he's done. He abandons the creature.

Victor's best friend brings him home. Meanwhile, the creature wanders around. He observes people and their ways. Because of the

way he looks, the poor hideous creature is rejected
by all of the humans he meets. He is nameless
and lonely, but very strong. He teaches himself
to talk and read. Then he hunts down Victor
Frankenstein.

The creature wants Victor to build him a
partner—a female mate. Frankenstein agrees at
first, then tears apart the experiment. In revenge,
the monster kills many of Victor's loved ones,

including his wife on their wedding night.
Frankenstein then chases his monster over great
distances—across Europe and up to the Arctic.
There, Victor, nearly dead, is rescued by a polar
explorer, Captain Robert Walton. He tells his
story to Captain Walton. The monster boards
the ship just as Victor Frankenstein dies, and
tells his story, too. When he is finished with his
tale, the creature jumps ship and disappears into
the darkness on a sheet of
floating ice.

Prometheus

The *Prometheus* of Mary Shelley's title was a Greek and Roman god—and a thief! He stole fire from the gods. In some myths, he secretly hides the flame in a plant stalk and gives it to humans. Then he teaches them about science and culture. In other myths, Prometheus sculpts the first people from clay and uses fire to bring them to life.

Prometheus was punished by the god Zeus for helping humans. He was chained to a rock. An eagle pecked out his liver every day. Every night it grew back and every morning the bird returned.

Some of the themes of this myth—creation, a quest for scientific knowledge, and punishment— are important ideas in Mary Shelley's novel.

This is the basic plot of Mary Shelley's story. Of course there are far more characters, details, and plot twists in the actual book. Mary told her story in a complicated style, using three different narrators—people who are telling the story: Captain Robert Walton, Victor Frankenstein, and the monster.

Frankenstein begins with the letters Captain Walton writes about his voyage to his sister in England. He explains how he spotted a dark shape far-off in the remote landscape. It appeared to be a huge man-like creature traveling by dog sled across the ice. Then he writes of how he came to find Victor Frankenstein the next day. He washed up against Walton's boat on a piece of ice. He was freezing, starving, and ill.

Victor Frankenstein then becomes the narrator. He tells of his experiments, the monster, the murders, finding his creature in the Alps, and swearing revenge. His story is the main part of

Frankenstein; or, The Modern Prometheus.

The novel then returns to Captain Walton's letters. But one of them describes the monster entering the captain's cabin. He is standing over the body of Victor Frankenstein, who has just died. Now the creature begins to tell his side of the story.

This style of writing was very popular in Mary Shelley's time. Having a story told by someone who heard it from someone else was meant to make it sound more believable. Three narrators make the novel interesting and exciting. Having three different storytellers also allows the author to present different points of view.

And Mary had many ideas she wanted to convey in her novel!

Frankenstein's Castle

In late summer 1814, Mary and Percy Shelley had taken a boat ride on the Rhine River. They passed the medieval ruins of the stone towers of Frankenstein Castle near Darmstadt, Germany. Its name means "rock of the Franks." (The Franks were Germanic people of the area.) Mary may have been inspired by the castle. She may have heard legends about Johann Dippel, who had once lived there. Dippel had searched for an "elixir of life," a magic potion of immortality. And he may have experimented on corpses.

What he ended up creating was Dippel's Oil—a smelly liquid made from boiled animal parts and bones. It didn't make you live forever, but it was a very good insect repellant.

CHAPTER 3
Scary Science

In her introduction to *Frankenstein*, Mary Shelley says she wanted to write a story that would "make the reader dread to look around, to curdle the blood, and quicken the beating of the heart." She accomplished that, and more. She also wrote one of the first science-fiction novels.

Mary was interested in books and ideas on many subjects. As her father said, "her desire of knowledge is great." And there were plenty of new ideas in the air.

In the early 1800s, theories about electricity and magnetism were debated. Biology and chemistry expanded as scientific fields. Steam was transformed into a source of power. This brought about many new industries and inventions.

Mary and her friends took part in lively discussions about all of these new scientific developments. She also read many

John Milton

important poems, like *Paradise Lost* by John Milton. In this 1667 epic poem, Milton explores the complicated relationship between God and his creations.

Mary Shelley drew on all these influences when she wrote *Frankenstein*.

Her main character is a scientist. (She did not use this word, though. The term *scientist* was not used until 1834.) She wrote her book in a way that makes the scientific parts sound realistic. This is remarkable because she doesn't exactly describe *how* Frankenstein brings his creature to life. But she does write a lot about what happens after he does.

Grave Business

The most important tool for a nineteenth-century scientist studying the human body was . . . a body! But those weren't always easy to come by. In an age with no refrigeration, corpses did not last long. Also, most people at the time thought it was wrong to dissect or cut up human bodies, even for scientific reasons.

There was money to be earned by digging up the newly dead and selling their bodies. The people who did this were called "ghouls," "body snatchers," or "resurrection men." They worked in secret to "resurrect" or bring back the dead—though not to life.

In England, the Anatomy Act of 1832 made it legal for scientists and doctors to study donated corpses. This cut down on grave robbing.

Frankenstein is a horror story. But it is also a highly imaginative story where people, science, and technology clash. That makes it science fiction.

In her novel, Shelley raises important questions: What is right or wrong in the search for knowledge? What responsibility do scientists have for their actions? Where did the spark of life come from?

People are still looking for the answers to these questions—and still reading *Frankenstein*. Mary Shelley turned what started as a short story into a book for all time!

A Shocking Idea

In the 1790s, Italian scientist Luigi Galvani made a dead frog's leg twitch by touching it with copper wires and an iron plate. In 1803, 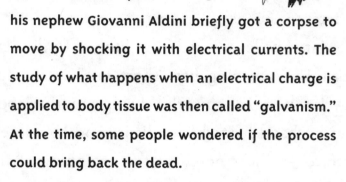 his nephew Giovanni Aldini briefly got a corpse to move by shocking it with electrical currents. The study of what happens when an electrical charge is applied to body tissue was then called "galvanism." At the time, some people wondered if the process could bring back the dead.

Mary Shelley would have first heard about the electrical current experiments called galvanism as a child. It was also a topic of discussion among the 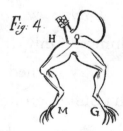 guests at the Villa Diodati in the summer of 1816. Shelley mentions the idea in her introduction to *Frankenstein*.

CHAPTER 4
Frankenstein Is Published

Frankenstein has three main narrators. It was also published three different times in three different versions.

Mary Shelley worked from June 1816 through April 1817 turning her "short tale" into a full novel. (She did all this while being a mother, too.) Her husband helped her edit it. And he wrote a preface—a short note—at the beginning of the book.

Two publishers rejected the manuscript. A third, Lackington, Allen & Co., published *Frankenstein; or, The Modern Prometheus* on January 1, 1818, in three volumes. Only five hundred copies were printed. Mary earned a little more than forty-one British pounds, around

$4,000 in today's money. Her name did not even appear on her own book!

Frankenstein received mixed reviews. Some people assumed Mary's husband wrote it. One critic called it "the foulest Toadstool"! But the book was a success.

In 1823, a play inspired by *Frankenstein*  opened in London. It was very popular. Mary Shelley was not involved with the play. She was not even in England when it opened. But her father thought it was a good time to publish a new version of her novel. William Godwin arranged for a two-volume *Frankenstein* to be published. The title page now included the author's name, Mary Wollstonecraft Shelley.

On Halloween, October 31, 1831, the final version of *Frankenstein* was published. It was a single volume that included a new introduction by the author. Mary had revised the text. By this time, she had lived through many tragedies. She had lost three children and a half sister. Her beloved husband, Percy Bysshe Shelley, had drowned. She was a widow with one child and constant money worries. Perhaps these facts influenced the changes Mary made to her book.

Mary Shelley's notebooks, in which she originally wrote *Frankenstein*, do not survive. The 1818 three-volume edition is a rare collector's item. The 1831 version of *Frankenstein* is the one used most often by modern publishers.

Romantic Goths

Frankenstein is sometimes called a gothic novel. Gothic novels are about the mysterious and the supernatural. They are often set in remote castles or monasteries. They feature dark secrets, mysterious villains, ghosts, even madness. These stories rarely end well! They were most popular from around 1750 to 1850.

Mary Shelley's novel also has elements of a movement called Romanticism, which emphasized the importance of emotions. It celebrated the power of nature. According to the Romantics, scientists should seek to understand, not control nature. Lord Byron and Percy Bysshe Shelley are two of the best-known English Romantic writers.

CHAPTER 5
Beyond the Book

At the end of the novel *Frankenstein*, the creature says, "He is dead who called me into being; and when I shall be no more, the very remembrance of us both will speedily vanish."

Not very likely! The monster and his maker live on and on and on!

In the forty or so years after it was printed, Mary Shelley's book sold around eight thousand copies. But more people knew of the story because they had seen it performed as a play in a theater. During the nineteenth century, the Frankenstein story had been kept alive onstage.

That changed in the twentieth century. Nearly one hundred years after Mary's book was published, her monster came "alive" in a new medium: movies!

Motion Pictures

Movies were first called motion pictures. Actually, the pictures are *not* moving. A movie is an optical illusion, something that tricks the eye.

A motion picture is many, many still images that have been photographed with a special camera. Movie cameras take a series of pictures very quickly. Each of these pictures is called a frame. The film of these frames runs through a movie projector so fast that what you see on the screen appears to move. (If you've ever played with a flip-book, you've seen this effect, too.)

Several inventions made motion pictures possible.

Thomas Alva Edison, the inventor of the phonograph, had his famous laboratory in West Orange, New Jersey. There, one of his assistants, William Kennedy Dickson, helped invent the motion-picture camera in 1888. Then George Eastman, a businessman and inventor in Rochester, New York, began manufacturing a new type of film in 1889. This was a roll of paper coated with

Thomas Alva Edison

a special chemical plastic. It was flexible and long-lasting. It was perfect for a motion-picture camera.

In 1893, the Edison Company built America's first movie studio at their lab in New Jersey. It was a dark, one-room building with a movable roof so that the sun could provide the lighting needed to shoot films inside. The whole building rotated on tracks to follow the sunlight.

America's first movie studio

Edison Studios made the very first Frankenstein movie. Their 1910 film was around thirteen minutes long. It was filmed in only three or four days.

The studio advertised the film as adapted from "Mrs. Shelley's famous story." They claimed they had removed all the "repulsive" or gross parts from this "weird tale" for the sake of the audience. In reality, the filmmakers changed quite a bit!

In Edison's *Frankenstein*, a mad scientist mixes special potions in a giant, bubbling pot. A skeleton emerges from the goop and turns into a bug-eyed, frizzy-haired fiend. The filmmakers

actually used a human skeleton to achieve this special effect. They set it on fire, photographed the burning bones, then ran the film backward to create the scene.

Each of the Edison Studios moviemakers did more than one job. The director also wrote the script. The actor who played the monster did his own creepy makeup and costumes. And even the film was reused.

Edison Studios would have made only about forty prints of the movie to distribute for screenings. Their *Frankenstein* wasn't all that popular. It might have looked a bit old-fashioned compared to other movies being made at the time. Or some people may not have liked the idea of watching a monster being "created" by a man.

After the screenings, the movie theaters returned the *Frankenstein* film prints to the studio. The films were stripped of their valuable chemical plastic and discarded. For a long time, this amazing early movie was thought to be lost. Most people believed that all the copies had been stripped clean and reused. However, in the 1970s, one rare copy was found among the films of a private collector. And you can find it online.

Edison Studios' film may have been the first—but the most *famous* Frankenstein movie was yet to come.

CHAPTER 6
Horror Goes to Hollywood

Early motion pictures were black and white, and they did not have sound. When filming a silent movie, it wasn't a problem if people made noise in the studio.

Carl Laemmle

Therefore, Carl Laemmle could invite the public to come visit Universal City Studios, his huge movie studio ranch in North Hollywood,

California. The 230-acre studio included a mountain range, a river, an artificial lake, and six enormous film stages. People could picnic or sit in the bleachers and watch movies being filmed—if they were willing to pay a quarter admission fee. (For a nickel more, they got a lunch!)

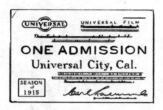

Laemmle was a German immigrant who opened one of the first motion picture theaters in Chicago, Illinois. He went on to become a movie producer. And in 1912, he joined forces with eight other producers to create the Universal Film Manufacturing Company. Usually just called Universal, it was the first "big" studio in Hollywood. Laemmle became president of this new movie studio. Eventually, he bought out his other partners.

When Universal City Studios opened in 1915, it was the world's largest movie-production studio. Laemmle insisted Universal pay for and distribute all of its movies. They did not ask for loans or outside investors. They also did not own movie theaters.

At this time, movies were changing from silent films to "talkies." Adding sound to movies meant that studios had to be equipped for all kinds of sound recording. It became difficult for Universal to compete with other movie studios that had better equipment, and that owned their own movie theaters.

By the 1920s, Laemmle's son, Carl Jr., was an executive at his father's company. He had bold ideas about how to make Universal Studios rise above the competition. Carl Jr. invested in new sound equipment. He bought movie theaters in which to screen Universal's films. But most importantly: He produced horror movies.

In the 1930s, nearly 65 percent of all Americans went to the movies every week. That's more than eighty million people! They showed up to see the short film newsreels about current events, followed by the movies that entertained—and sometimes *scared*—them.

And when it came to scary movies, Universal was king.

Universal had already made a few successful silent movies with a touch of horror. In the 1920s, *The Hunchback of Notre Dame* and *The Phantom of the Opera* were big hits for the studio. But the elder Laemmle thought horror movies were

Carl Laemmle Jr.

"distasteful." He left that side of the business to his son. However, Carl Laemmle Jr. thought there could be something profitable in the business of horror movies.

The first sound horror film made at Universal was *Dracula*. It was based on a stage play of the popular book by Bram Stoker. Bela Lugosi, a Hungarian actor who was also the star of the play, was cast as the "undead" Count Dracula who can mysteriously turn into a bat. The film was produced by Carl Jr.

Dracula opened in New York City on February 12, 1931. More than fifty thousand people saw it there in just the first few days! Thousands more flocked to movie theaters across the country when it opened nationwide soon after.

This was good news for Carl Jr. and his company. Business had been down for Universal by several million dollars. The younger Laemmle realized the earning potential of horror movies. Nine months after *Dracula*'s sensational opening,

Universal brought another classic novel to life on the big screen. The movie studio and Mary Shelley's monster were about to make headlines.

Movies Get Cool

The first motion pictures were silent—and the first movie theaters were hot! The screening rooms were dark and windowless. It was difficult to sell movie tickets in the summer, especially in the warmer parts of the country.

In 1925, a young engineer convinced the Paramount movie company to let him install his new invention in a movie theater they were building in Times Square, New York City. His name was Willis Carrier. His invention was an air-conditioning system.

Over the next five years, Carrier had air conditioning

installed in three hundred movie theaters across the
country that advertised "Cooled by Refrigeration"
or "Scientifically Air-Conditioned" buildings.

Air conditioning also became important to
the moviemaking process. Studios really did need
"quiet on the set." Film stages had to be kept closed
off from unwanted noise. But moviemaking also
required big, hot lights. Air conditioning kept the
movie sets—and the actors—cool during shooting.

CHAPTER 7
The Monster Is Loose!

In the fall of 1931, a movie poster stopped people in their tracks. They stared into a pair of dead eyes in a large, misshapen head. Big letters scrawled across the poster screamed, "Warning! The Monster Is Loose!"

They were looking at the first "teaser" in the history of movie publicity. Teasers are ads that make people curious about something. They are meant to draw in audiences. And in November 1931, Universal wanted to attract moviegoers to its newest horror film . . . *Frankenstein*.

The year before, Carl Laemmle Jr. had hired James Whale, a British director. Most of Whale's experience was in directing stage plays. In the early days of movies with sound, many actors were hired from the theater, too. "Talkies" had sound, of course. Stage actors were used to speaking their lines, while silent movie stars were not. Universal even relied on the theater for scripts for their first horror movies. The writers for both the *Dracula* and *Frankenstein* movies started with theater adaptations. The horror stories had been transformed from books to plays to movies!

Name That Monster!

Mary Shelley did not give the monster a name in her novel. In the book, he is referred to as "creature," "fiend," "devil," "demon," "wretch," "being," "ogre," or just plain "it." Frankenstein is the last name of the creator of the monster: Victor Frankenstein.

When plays inspired by Mary's book were first produced, the monster was also nameless. This character was represented by "_____" in the list of actors and the roles they played.

The title credits for Universal's early Frankenstein movies—the first seven—read "The Monster . . . ?" Although some theater productions started calling the monster Frankenstein in the 1820s, Universal didn't use Frankenstein as the name of the monster until 1943.

THE PLAYERS

Henry Frankenstein ... COLIN CLIVE

Elizabeth .... MAE CLARKE

Victor Moritz .... JOHN BOLES

The Monster .... ?

Doctor Waldman .. EDWARD VAN SLOAN

Baron Frankenstein .... FREDERICK KERR

Fritz .... DWIGHT FRYE

The Burgomaster .... LIONEL BELMORE

Little Marta .... MARILYN HARRIS

Director James Whale chose the actors for the *Frankenstein* movie. When it came to the monster, he made a now-legendary decision!

Boris Karloff was a good choice to play the creature. He had starred in many silent films. Actors in these films had to be skilled at showing emotions through facial expressions and body movements. In Whale's film, the monster was not going to speak very many lines, but he would have to be very expressive. Karloff would have to "show" what he couldn't "tell"!

James Whale

Movie Makeup

Everybody knows what Frankenstein looks like: a flap of hair over a big forehead, a heavy brow, scarred green skin, and, of course, the bolts in the neck.

Mary Shelley didn't create *this* monstrous look—movie makeup artist Jack Pierce did! Pierce did such

Jack Pierce

an incredible job that Universal copyrighted the monster's look. (This means the makeup design legally belongs to the studio. It can't be copied without the studio's permission.)

Pierce asked Boris Karloff to remove a dental plate—an old-fashioned type of dentures—he wore. This caused the actor's cheek to cave in a little. It made his face look lopsided. The makeup artist then went to work. He created the creature's oversize head using cotton, putty, and a chemical solution that causes wrinkles when it dries. He spread green greasepaint over the actor's face and hands. (The green-tinted makeup showed up better on black-and-white film.) He painted the actor's fingernails black and styled a wig to square off his head. It took Pierce about four hours a day to turn Boris Karloff into a monster!

One publicity photograph shows Karloff in his costume with a white cloth bag over his head. Jack Pierce is leading him by the hand to the film stage. This was the studio's way of keeping the monster's chilling look a secret!

Universal's *Frankenstein* movie did not follow the plot of Mary Shelley's book very closely. The names of some characters were changed. Other characters were added, like a hunchbacked lab assistant named Fritz. Dr. Frankenstein is much more of a mad scientist than he is in the book. And the creature acts like a monster because he was mistakenly given a stolen "abnormal" brain instead of a normal one.

Mary Shelley never fully described how her monster came to life. But that is the movie's most famous scene. Frankenstein and his assistant work in a secret lab filled with bubbling glass tubes and complicated electrical wiring, coils, and switches. Dr. Frankenstein is assembling body parts stolen from graves. His large, man-like creation is unseen. It is wrapped in cloth and lying on a table. The table rises up through the roof into a powerful lightning storm. The whole lab is flashing, buzzing, and sparking. When the

Fritz

table comes back down, Frankenstein leans over, sees the creature's hand move, and shouts, "It's alive. IT'S ALIVE!"—one of the most famous movie lines of all time.

Boris Karloff's performance made audiences feel sorry for the monster. At first, he is just a confused and frightened creature. He can't talk. His outstretched arms and hands make him look like he is pleading for help. The creature doesn't mean to cause such damage and destruction. But he does. Everybody is afraid of him. They are horrified by the way he looks. In the end, he really *does* act like a monster.

Frankenstein cost about $250,000 to make. The movie opened in New York City on December 4, 1931. At the beginning of the film, one of the actors appears onscreen with a friendly warning from Carl Laemmle Jr.: The movie "may shock you" or "horrify you." The actor adds that if "you do not care to subject your nerves to such a strain, now's your chance to, uh, well—we warned you!"

But nobody paid attention to the warning!

Audiences packed theaters, ready to be thrilled. Universal's *Frankenstein* earned $12 million, which would be more than $170 million today.

Chapter 8
Frankenstein Returns . . .
More Than Once

James Whale originally filmed a fiery ending to *Frankenstein* in which the monster kills his creator and then dies himself in a blaze set by angry villagers. But audiences who watched an early preview wanted a happier Hollywood ending. Universal decided to give it to them: Dr. Frankenstein escapes and is reunited with his fiancée. The creature falls through a burning windmill into a flooded pit.

Or does he . . . ?

Universal's horror films were very successful. Frankenstein returned in several more movies. And so did some of the cast.

Whale directed the first sequel, *Bride of Frankenstein*, in 1935. Boris Karloff was back to play the monster. (This time, he got his name in the credits as "Karloff." The bride, however, was listed only as "The Monster's Mate . . . ?")

Bride of Frankenstein opens with the Shelleys and Lord Byron together in a fancy room in a mansion. A storm rages outside. The actress

playing Mary reveals that her novel wasn't the end of the story. She asks the two men, "Would you like to hear what happens after that?" And so the film begins.

The creature rises up out of the watery pit in the smoking ruins. Jack Pierce had singed the wig and added makeup burns to the creature. Boris

Karloff still played the role with compassion. The monster lives with a blind hermit who plays the violin. He learns to speak. He loves music. He has a friend. But in the end, that friend is driven away by horrified hunters. The monster does not want to be alone. He searches for his creator. He wants Dr. Frankenstein to make him a friend and a partner.

Kenneth Strickfaden, the special-effects wizard who built the lab for *Frankenstein*, did it again for the 1935 movie. Jack Pierce created the startling hair and makeup for the female monster. He modeled her look after a sculpture of the famous Egyptian queen Nefertiti. The monster's dark hair is teased straight up from her head. It has a white streak that looks like a lightning bolt. She has long eyelashes and a beautiful profile—except for the jagged stiches all around her neck and ears.

The creation scene in *Bride of Frankenstein* is as electric as that in the first film. But the story quickly becomes a tragedy. The monster moves toward his mate. His arms are out and welcoming. He says the first word he ever learned, "friend."

His bride hisses and screams.

Karloff's monster is heartbroken: "She hate me. Like others." He wrecks the lab but spares Dr. Frankenstein. A tear rolls down the monster's scarred cheek, right before he pulls the switch that blows up the whole building.

But that is still not "The End."

Universal brought out *Son of Frankenstein* in 1939. Boris Karloff returned as the monster. But this time he was quiet and even more dangerous. He was being bossed around by an angry, deformed grave robber. Bela Lugosi, who had

become famous as Dracula, played Ygor (say: EE-gor), the grave robber.

The movie was a big success.

Ygor

Lugosi's evil Ygor was back in the 1942 film, *The Ghost of Frankenstein*. But there was a new monster in town. Boris Karloff did not want to play the role again. The job went to Lon Chaney Jr., who had been the furry star of *The Wolf Man* just a year earlier. In an exciting early scene, Chaney's monster arises from a sulfur

pit. *The Ghost of Frankenstein* didn't have the big budget of the earlier movies. It was also the last Universal film that featured the Frankenstein monster as a solo star.

Monster Stars

Universal's horror movies featured some pretty big Hollywood stars.

Boris Karloff (1887–1969) appeared in more than 150 films, including *The Mummy* in 1932. He also voiced the Grinch in the cartoon of Dr. Seuss's *How the Grinch Stole Christmas*. Karloff's real name was William Henry Pratt. He was born in London, England.

Elsa Lanchester (1902–1986) played Mary Shelley at the beginning of *Bride of Frankenstein*. Then she changed her fancy gown for a full-bandage body wrap to play the monster's mate at the end of the movie. She was born in London, England.

Bela Lugosi (1882–1956) was born Béla Ferenc Dezső Blaskó in what was then Lugos, Hungary. He kept his own strong accent when he played the vampire Count Dracula and other villains in Universal horror movies.

Lon Chaney Jr. (1906–1973) inherited his monster genes! His father was a well-known star of silent horror movies. Chaney Jr. became famous for playing a werewolf, Frankenstein's monster, a mummy, and a vampire. The actor's real name was Creighton Tull Chaney. He was born in Oklahoma City.

Universal's next film, *Frankenstein Meets the Wolf Man* in 1943, was the very first time the studio used the name Frankenstein to mean the

creature. Horror fans were familiar with the names in the cast, but this time, the roles were switched. Now Bela Lugosi played Frankenstein's monster.

Lon Chaney Jr. went back to being the Wolf Man. The movie was successful. So Universal's next horror film upped the number of monster characters.

In 1944, *House of Frankenstein* brought together Dracula, the Wolf Man, and Frankenstein's creation—back to being called just "the monster." This time Boris Karloff did appear—but in the role of a mad scientist. Movie fans didn't seem to mind these changes.

Four years later, Universal planned a new movie that combined horror and comedy. Bud Abbott and Lou Costello were popular comedians who worked together. Their famous routine is called "Who's on First?" The Frankenstein, Dracula, and Wolf Man characters were also crowd-pleasers. Why not put them all together?

Abbott and Costello Meet Frankenstein came out in 1948. The monster and the Wolf Man still looked the way Jack Pierce originally designed them. But by this time, a new makeup artist had figured out how to make rubber masks for both creatures. No more four hours a day in the makeup chair!

For seventeen years, from 1931 until 1948, horror movies were popular and successful for Universal. And Frankenstein's monster towered over all the other film creatures!

Choose Your Own . . .

There were many differences between Mary Shelley's novel 📖 and Universal's movies 🎥.

- **Victor Frankenstein**

  📖 Curious university student; best friend is named Henry

  🎥 Mad scientist; renamed Dr. Henry Frankenstein

- **The monster**

  📖 No name; yellow skin; teaches himself to speak and read French; talks a lot about the meaning of life, love, and revenge

  🎥 No name at first, then called Frankenstein; green skin; not much of a talker

- **Lab assistant**

  📖 None, Victor is a one-man show

  🎥 Usually a hunchback, dwarf, or disfigured

fellow; called Fritz in the first movie,
but Ygor is the name everybody now
remembers

• How monster comes to life
📝 Not really explained: "instruments of life"
used to "infuse a spark of being"
🎥 Lightning bolts and lots of electrical gizmos

• "It's alive! IT'S ALIVE!"
📝 Never said
🎥 #42 on the American Film Institute's "100
Greatest Movie Quotes of All Time"

• End of story
📝 COLD! Victor Frankenstein chases the
monster to the Arctic. Victor dies. Monster
floats away on a raft in the freezing waters.
🎥 HOT! Dr. Frankenstein always escapes.
Monster is always doomed to a fiery or
explosive end.

CHAPTER 9
It's *Still* Alive!

No matter what really happened at the end of Mary Shelley's book, she created a monster that truly never died. Her Frankenstein story has inspired many, many other creations.

There are more than two hundred Frankenstein films. The British movie studio Hammer Films made several gory ones— in color! In these low-budget films, Victor Frankenstein is a baron, a cruel aristocrat who's secretly a mad scientist.

Peter Cushing played Baron Frankenstein in six of Hammer's seven Frankenstein films. The first one, *The Curse of Frankenstein*, made in 1957, also starred Christopher Lee as the creature. One reason the studio liked Lee for

Peter Cushing

the role was because he was tall! (Cushing and Lee appeared in more than twenty films together!)

Christopher Lee

In the 1970s, two funny monster-inspired movies came out. The movie spoof *Young Frankenstein* featured the original lab equipment from Universal's 1931 film. *The Rocky Horror Picture Show* is a musical comedy about Dr. Frank-N-Furter. It was one of the first movies in the United States to inspire cosplay. That's when fans dress up and appear as their favorite characters.

And in 2012, a popular animated movie, *Frankenweenie*, featuring a boy named Victor who brings his pet dog back to life, was released.

On Location

"Little Europe" is part of the tram ride at Universal Studios. It goes through some of the sets from *Frankenstein* and *Bride of Frankenstein*. These sets were used in village scenes in both movies. The tour originally featured the actual movie sets from the 1930s. But they were destroyed in a fire in 1967 and have since been rebuilt.

Meanwhile, the monster wasn't just a film star. It was also a TV character in two series that were originally broadcast from 1964 to 1966. *The Munsters* was a popular comedy about a family of monsters. Herman Munster, the big, goofy father,

Herman Munster

Lurch

was a Frankenstein look-alike. So was Lurch, the butler on *The Addams Family*. Like the Universal monster, he mostly just growled and groaned, except for his famous phrase: "You rang?"

Even *The Simpsons* has featured Frankenstein themes in several of the show's annual "Treehouse of Horror" Halloween episodes. The Simpson family also dressed up as characters in the Munster family!

Frankenstein's monster has appeared in more than 650 comic books. From 1945 to 1954, Prize Comics published *The New Adventures of Frankenstein*. It was a horror comic, but later

issues featured the monster living in a small town with other monster neighbors. There's a *Classics Illustrated* comic of Mary Shelley's novel. And the creature has also been seen in comics with Captain America, the Flintstones, and even Archie!

Toy stores sell all kinds of dolls and action figures inspired by the monster. And every Halloween, there are Frankenstein masks and costumes on the shelves.

Even the United States Postal Service liked the monster enough to issue a Boris Karloff Frankenstein stamp in 1997, as part of their Universal Monsters series.

The word Frankenstein or the slang "franken-" is used today. It can mean something that has been scientifically altered, or changed, or modified. For example, some people call animals that have been bred a certain way "frankenfood." The slang can also refer to something unusual in nature, like the "frankenfish," a fish that can walk on land.

"Monster Mash"

    In 1962, the number one pop song was a "graveyard smash." It was called "Monster Mash." It is about a Frankenstein-like monster that comes to life and dances "the mash." The song was recorded by Bobby "Boris" Pickett and his backup band The Crypt-Kickers with rattling chains and squeaky coffin-lid sound effects. Pickett sang in a deep voice to sound like Boris Karloff. People danced to the hit song with stiff and jerky movements, like the way Frankenstein's monster moves. The song is still a Halloween favorite.

Universal's *Frankenstein* even inspired some real science. Dr. Jean Rosenbaum watched the 1931 movie as a child. He never forgot the lab scenes. The image of "sparking" the monster to life stayed with him. As a medical student, he wondered if you could use electricity to get a stopped heart to beat again. Rosenbaum went on to invent the first heart pacemaker in 1951. It does just that.

Young Mary Shelley wrote that she wanted to create something that would "awaken thrilling horror." She succeeded!

The impact of Frankenstein has spanned centuries, countries, and cultures. Shelley would likey be astonished by all that her book has inspired and flattered by the imposing statue of her monster in Geneva.

And she'd probably love to see a Frankenstein movie!

Bibliography

*Books for young readers

Failing, Christopher. *Frankenstein: The First Two Hundred Years.*
London: Reel Art Press, 2017.

Frankenstein: Complete Legacy Collection. DVD. Universal City,
CA: Universal Pictures Home Entertainment, 2014.

*Frith, Margaret. *Who Was Thomas Alva Edison?* New York:
Penguin Workshop, 2005.

*Goddu, Krystyna Poray. *Movie Monsters: From Godzilla to
Frankenstein.* Minneapolis, MN: Lerner Publications, 2017.

Gordon, Charlotte. *Romantic Outlaws: The Extraordinary Lives
of Mary Wollstonecraft & Mary Shelley.* New York: Random
House, 2015.

Neibaur, James L. *The Monster Movies of Universal Studios.*
Lanham, MD: Rowman & Littlefield, 2017.

Searle Dawley, J., director. *Frankenstein (1910).* Edison
Manufacturing Co., 1910, www.youtube.com/
watch?v=N2N93pcKFL8.

Shelley, Mary. *Frankenstein: The 1818 Text.* New York: Penguin,
2018.

*Shelley, Mary. *Gris Grimly's Frankenstein.* Illustrated by Gris
Grimly. New York: Balzer + Bray/HarperCollins, 2015.

Shelley, Mary. *The New Annotated Frankenstein.* Edited by Leslie
S. Klinger. New York, New York: Liveright Publishing/W.W.
Norton & Company, Ltd. 2017.

Websites

www.poetryfoundation.org/poets/mary-wollstonecraft-shelley
www.shelleygodwinarchive.org